YO-BXY-390

Kid's Say the Cutest Things About Dad!

Kid's Say the Cutest Things About Dad
ISBN 1-57757-281-5
Copyright © 1997 by Trade Life Books, Inc.
P.O. Box 55325
Tulsa, OK 74155

Compiled by Dandi Daley Mackall

Introduction

Ever wonder what dads are made of? Now find out the often hilarious and sometimes touching truths straight from the mouths of the world's top authorities on dads...kids!

This delightful book is sure to entertain you with the honest and refreshingly open comments that can only come from a child. You'll find yourself smiling as you turn each page.

After reading this book you need no longer wonder what it takes to be a dad! The following pages are filled with a candid honesty that reveals not only the lighter side, but often times the touching reality of the special relationship which exists between children and their dad.

It is sure to provide family entertainment as you get an inside glimpse of what those children are really thinking!

Why Did God Make Fathers?

- So there'd be somebody
around to take care of us
when God was busy.

- Somebody's got to earn
our allowance!

Why Did God Make Fathers?

- To put worms on your fishing hook.

- To help mothers when they get too tired of doing everything.

How Did God Make Daddies?

– God used glue
and dirt and
several drills
and it took
thirty days.

Name The Secret Ingredient
For Fathers.

- Vinegar.

- Salad or macaroni, I can't
  remember which.

Who Was The First Father?

- Time. Father Time.

- George Washington. He was
the first American father anyway.

Who Was The First Father?

- Adam. Only it didn't turn
  out so good.

- Chuck. You know, Chuck!

What Ingredients Are Fathers Made Of?

– Daddies are made of
baseballs – basketballs
– and footballs.
Oh – and my uncle
is also made of golf.

What Ingredients Are Fathers Made Of?

- Sugar and spice and money.

- Dads are mostly made of tease.

Why Did God Give You Your Dad And Not Some Other Dad?

- Because my mom likes him a real lot.

- He's around our house a lot. And we were both born loving basketball.

Why Did God Give You Your Dad And Not Some Other Dad?

- God picked my dad out just for me because God has a very good sense of humor.

- 'Cause he looks just like me and my brothers.

Why Did God Give You Your Dad And Not Some Other Dad?

– My dad went through Vietnam and jumped out of planes eight times. God thought he could handle a daughter.

What Did Your Dad Want To Be When He Grew Up?

- My dad could never make up his mind if he wanted to be an astronaut or a cow-milker. So he ended up a sheriff.

- He wanted to be an albino fireman.

How Has Life Changed Since Your Dad Was A Little Boy?

- We can drive cars now. When Dad was little — I don't think they invented cars yet. They'd only invented horses.

- Nobody back then had a driver's license.

How Has Life Changed Since Your Dad Was A Little Boy?

- It was harder for kids to study back in those days because they didn't have knowledge yet.

- For one thing, he used to live in my grandma's house.
Now he lives with us.
That's a big change.

How Has Life Changed Since Your Dad Was A Little Boy?

– They all wore old-fashioned clothes. No modern clothes allowed.

What Kind Of Little Boy
Was Your Dad?

- Did you ever see
Dennis the Menace?

- My dad says he was the nicest
kid in the whole world and never
got into trouble. My grandma
says he was a bad, bad boy.
I don't know who to believe.

What Kind Of Little Boy Was Your Dad?

- He used to cheat and
  lie sometimes but
  now he's a lawyer.

- My dad was a tattle-tale.
  He used to put worms in
  my grandma's bed and
  then tell on himself.

How Did Your Dad Meet Your Mom?

- I think they met at
a family reunion.

- My mom and dad met at
this party that went on for
a year...in the sixties.

How Did Your Dad Meet Your Mom?

– They already knew each other. Then my mom got way dressed up one day and my dad all of a sudden noticed she was alive.

What Did Dad Need To Know About Mom Before He Married Her?

- He needed to know how old she was, but she never told him.

- If she had a personality or not.

Why Did Your Dad Marry Your Mom?

- Because they both used to be beautiful, and they just didn't know what else they could do about it.

- God told them they had to marry or burn up. So, they got themselves married fast!

Why Did Your Dad Marry Your Mom?

- Because he didn't want to die by himself.

- I think he wanted to get away from his mom.

Why Did Your Dad Marry Your Mom?

– They got married
so they could have
the most cake
at the reception.

What Did Your Dad Do Before He Had Kids Of His Own?

- He had to boss around other kids, like his nieces and nephews, and sometimes strangers.

- He bought all kinds of stuff for his own self.

What Did Your Dad Do Before He Had Kids Of His Own?

- He played with his
tools a lot more than
he does now.

- They didn't let him go to
parent meetings at school or
read magazines for parents
or buy parent clothing.

What's The Difference Between Dads And Moms?

- If they're running for the car door in the rain, dads are supposed to hold it open, and moms are supposed to get in first.

- Dads argue louder and hardly ever have babies.

What's The Difference Between Dads And Moms?

- The biggest difference
  is their hair choices.
  Moms can have short
  hair or long hair.
  Dads can have short
  hair or no hair.

What Does It Mean
To Be A Real Man?

- A real man admits when
he's wrong. But, my dad
is never wrong.

- Being loyal to your
sports' team even when
they're real losers.

What Does It Mean
To Be A Real Man?

- It means you're very brave —
  even when your wife is
  really mad at you.

- Real men love dirt and
  getting dirty and never
  washing their hairs.

Who's The Boss At Your House?

- Whoever's got the
remote control!

- It's hard to tell because
my mom bosses our dog
around, and our dog
bosses my dad around.

Who's The Boss At Your House?

– My mom is the boss
of our house and
my dad is the boss
of our car.

How Can You Tell Who The Boss Is In Your Family?

- I just don't know. My dad yells, "I'll show you who's the boss around here!" But he never really does.

- My dad is boss...because Mom says so!

What Does Your Father Do All Day?

- He does other people's
dirty work better than they
do it themselves.

- I think he stands up all day at
work, because when he gets home
he can't do anything except sit.

What Does Your Father Do All Day?

- My dad mostly blows all day long at work.   He's a seller of musical instruments.

- He yells at people at work. At night, he yells at home.

What Does Your Dad Do
In His Spare Time?

– His favorite thing
he does every day is
watch old – old football
films of himself
and says, "Look!
Look at me there!"

What Does Your Dad Do
In His Spare Time?

- He builds rockets.
But it's a secret.

- He lies down on the couch
and closes his eyes and thinks.
But it sure looks like
sleeping to me.

What Does Your Dad Do After You Go To Bed?

- They don't think I know, but they get into the good food as soon as they think I'm asleep.

- Are you kidding? He goes to bed way before I do!

What Does Your Dad Do After You Go To Bed?

- He lifts and hits boards in the basement.

- It's pretty boring. He's got nothing to do but talk to my mom.

What Does Your Dad Do For Fun With His Friends?

– They watch football
or they play football
or they talk about
football or they dream
about football or they
make footballs.

What Does Your Dad Do For Fun With His Friends?

- They talk about the olden days when they were all heroes.

- My dad and his friends have the most fun doing stuff my mom gets really mad about for days.

What's The Difference Between Dads And Grandpas?

- Grandpas are already bald.

- It's like the difference between golf and putt putt.

How Would I Recognize Your Dad If I Saw Him?

- He doesn't look the same as he used to. Now, he has wrinkles between his eyebrows.
He's losing his hair and his sense of humor.

- He has four hairs, all black. But, he may be down to two if you don't see him soon.

How Would I Recognize Your Dad
If I Saw Him?

– My dad never – ever takes his shoes off. So you'd recognize him when all the daddies are asleep. Mine's the one with shoes on.

If Your Dad Were An Animal, What Animal Would He Be?

- A dog. He's very loyal but bites when necessary.

- I'll bet my daddy would be a chicken. He just loves eggs.

If Your Dad Were An Animal, What Animal Would He Be?

- A bald eagle.
Guess why.

- My dad would be a horse.
He's so good at giving piggy-back rides! Hmmm...maybe
he should be a pig.

Describe The Worlds Greatest Dad

- He would do stuff you want
  to do when he wants to be
  doing something else.

- He'd whip all the bullies and
  fling them to high heaven.

Describe The Worlds Greatest Dad

- He would let you
date before you're a
hundred years old.

More On The World's Greatest Dad

- The most greatest dad in the world wouldn't take his portable phone on our fishing trips.

- The world's greatest dad would watch cartoons on a Saturday morning with me.

More On The World's Greatest Dad

- The world's greatest dad
would take you to the movies
when your friends went but
didn't invite you to go with them.

- The greatest dad would
play girl games too.

Is Anything About Your Dad Perfect?

- He'd tell you —
his _car_ is perfect!

- His hair. He sprays it
so it won't even move!

Is Anything About Your Dad Perfect?

– My dad is almost perfectly round.

What Would It Take To Make Your Dad Perfect?

- A shower.

- Ten inches and one hundred pounds. I'd like him to be bigger than the biggest bully.

What Would It Take To Make Your Dad Perfect?

- It would take leaving his "peeper" at home when we're on vacation.

- He's almost perfect because he takes us lots of fun places. But he'd be more perfect if he just took me and left my brother and sister at home.

If You Could Change One Thing About Your Dad, What Would You Change?

- I'd make him my age, so we could be best buddies.

- I'd make him more needy so he needed my help more.

If You Could Change One Thing About Your Dad, What Would You Change?

– HiS Socks!

What's The Hardest Part About Being A Dad?

- You have to keep the same kids every day of your life. You can get new ones, but no exchanges.

- Getting up in the morning, as far as I can tell.

What's The Hardest Part About Being A Dad?

- Giving your blood at the office.

- The hardest thing about being a good dad is sharing the television set.

What's The Best Thing About Your Dad?

- He's so easy for me to beat at everything, even though he can beat everybody else.

- My dad trusts me to go get lost out in the woods all by myself.

What's The Best Thing About Your Dad?

- I just love it when my dad gives my mom flowers.

What Makes Your Dad Happy?

- Me and Mom.

- Chocolate on everything and credit cards.

What Makes Your Dad Happy?

- I don't get why, but he really likes taking naps with my mom.

- Big screen TV. That, and leaving him alone during ball games.

What Makes Your Dad Mad?

- Broken things and
  women drivers.

- When my brothers and sisters
  and me argue with fists.

What Makes Your Dad Mad?

– Lawnmowers!
He really gives them
a talking to!

What Makes Your Dad Mad?

- I'm not sure, because we have a lot of trouble telling the difference when he's mad or happy.

- Interrupting while he's yelling.

What Makes Your Dad Sad?

- Roadkill

- Kids getting too big to give
  their old dad a hug.

What Makes Your Dad Sad?

- Are you kidding?
Nothing makes my dad sad.

- When my mom won't let his
friends play at our house.

What Makes Your Dad Laugh?

– He thinks my mom's face is pretty funny.

What Makes Your Dad Laugh?

- Little stuff that I'm not
allowed to say.

- Things that aren't funny. `Cause
when my dad is laughing really
hard, my mom always says,
"You're not funny, Frank!"

If You Could Give Your Dad Any Gift In The World, What Would You Give Him?

- I'd like to give my dad a new watch, so he wouldn't come home so late.

- I'd give Daddy a finding-machine. He can never find where he left his glasses or his car keys or his briefcase.

If You Could Give Your Dad Any Gift In The World, What Would You Give Him?

- I'd give my dad a racetrack. He's just too fast for the freeway.

- I would give my dad a giraffe, because my dad is very tall. Then he could pet it without bending over.

If You Could Give Your Dad Any Gift In The World, What Would You Give Him?

— His very own bike...and the time to ride it.

What's The Nicest Thing Your Dad Ever Did For You?

- When my fish died, my dad flushed it down the toilet for me and tried to look really sad.

- He turns the volume down on the TV if I really want to talk to him.

What's The Nicest Thing Your Dad Ever Did For You?

- He quit work one day and got me to quit school so he could take me out to lunch.

- My dad taught me how to throw rocks at cars.

What's The Nicest Thing You Ever Did For Your Dad?

- I told him what my mommy was getting him for his birthday.

- I ate his candy so he wouldn't get unhealthy.

What's The Nicest Thing You Ever Did For Your Dad?

– I think it would have to be hugging him. He really needs my hugs.

What's The Nicest Thing You Ever Did For Your Dad?

- I cooked him hot peppers and squash.

- I always get things for him while he lies on the couch.

Would You Like To Trade Places With Your Dad?

- I wouldn't mind being a dad
but I wouldn't want any
of his kids.

- Yeah! I always wanted
the big TV chair.

Would You Like To Trade Places With Your Dad?

- Yes. Then I could reach my mom better.

- No thanks. Something tells me he would be a handful.

Would You Like To Trade Places With Your Dad?

– I would like to trade places with my dad. I think it's the only way I'm going to get a tree house.

How Do You Know
Your Dad Loves You?

- Would I be known as
"Daddy's girl" if he didn't?

- Whenever I get in fights,
he looks out the window
and roots for me.

How Do You Know Your Dad Loves You?

- Sometimes when I'm asleep, he kisses me anyway. And, he wouldn't have to, because I'd never know the difference. Now that's love.

- He came to my Christmas program, and it went on forever!

How Do You Know
Your Dad Loves You?

- Mommy told me so.

- He let me pick out what color I wanted my bedroom. And when I picked purple, he didn't back out.

Do You Want To Be A Dad When You Grow Up?

– Yes. I will be a dad. I will have five boys who will become a basketball team. I will be their coach.

Do You Want To Be A Dad When You Grow Up?

- I can't wait until I'm a dad and can drive a car and go on vacations. Only I don't want a buch of screaming kids in the back seat.

- No thank you. There's a lot that goes into being Dad — like kissing moms and bringing home bacon.

Do You Want To Be A Dad When You Grow Up?

- Tell me my other choices.

- OK. I'll be the dad. But, I decided when I'm Daddy I'm not having a "no-no chair". (I'll be bigger then, and I just don't think I'm going to need one.)

What Do You Think Your Dad Prays For You?

- He just tells God thanks a lot.

- He prays I won't wake up sick in the night. He hates that!

What Do You Think Your Dad Prays For You?

– Something about birds and bees. I think it's that they won't sting me.

What Do You Think Your Dad Prays For You?

- My dad tells God to bless me.
I think that means for God
to make me a good kid.

- He prays I won't get
lost or stolen.

What Do You Pray For Your Dad?

- When my dad goes to the flea market, I pray he wouldn't bring home fleas.

- When he was in the hospital with an operation, I prayed they wouldn't sew out of the lines.

What Do You Pray For Your Dad?

- Sometimes I pray he'd be just like my mom when he grows up.

- I pray that dad will live happily ever after.

Additional copies of this book and other titles in the *Kids Tell* series are available from your local bookstore.

Kids Say the Cutest Things About Moms

Kids Say the Cutest Things About Dads

Trade Life Books
Tulsa, Oklahoma